MW01204974

CELEBRATING EARTH DAY

PRESENTED BY

GOV. ZELL MILLER

AND MEMBERS OF THE

1998 GEORGIA LEGISLATURE

CELEBRATING EARTH DAY

A Sourcebook of
Activities and Experiments

by Robert Gardner

illustrations by
Sharon Lane Holm

The Millbrook Press
Brookfield, Connecticut

Photographs courtesy of:
NASA: p. 8; UPI/Bettmann: p. 14;
Greenpeace: pp. 26 (Zachary Singer),
54 (Merjenburgh), 68 (Sam Kittner).

Library of Congress Cataloging-in-Publication Data

Gardner, Robert, 1929–
Celebrating earth day: a sourcebook of activities and experiments/
by Robert Gardner.
p.   cm.
Includes bibliographical references and index.
Summary: Commemorates the annual anniversary of Earth Day and
suggests activities and experiments for learning more about the
earth and how to improve its condition.
ISBN 1-56294-070-8 (lib. bdg.)
1. Environmental protection—Experiments—Juvenile literature.
2. Environmental education—Activity programs—Juvenile literature.
3. Earth Day—Juvenile literature.   [1. Environmental protection.
2. Earth Day.]   I. Title.
TD170.2.G.37   1992
333.7—dc20   91-38297   CIP   AC

CONTENTS

INTRODUCTION

The Earth does not belong to man.
Man belongs to the Earth.
Man did not weave the web of life.
He is merely a strand in it.
Whatever he does to the web,
he does to himself.

Chief Seattle, Dwamish tribe

A FEW CENTURIES AGO most people thought the Earth was the center of the universe. After all, it seemed obvious that the moon, the stars, and even the sun circled the Earth each day. Today, we know that our planet is but a tiny speck in a vast and expanding universe. Although our Earth is minuscule on the scale of the universe, it is the only home we have. If it is to remain a safe and habitable place for our descendants, we must strive to keep its air, water, and soil clean and unpolluted.

It is fitting that each year one day, April 22, is set aside to celebrate our planet, the only place in the universe known to have living creatures on its surface. The first such "Earth Day" was held in 1970. It consisted of a nationwide teach-in on college campuses to make people aware of environmental issues. The idea caught on, and Earth Days now involve more action than words. Many people spend the day cleaning up beaches, parks, and communities. They plant trees, organize plans to recycle and compost, attend Earth Fairs, and become involved in a variety of other activities related to improving the environment. It's fun, enlightening, and helpful to do these kinds of things on

Earth Day. But our concerns about the Earth must not be limited to one day a year. Caring for the Earth must be an ongoing concern for all of us.

No one alone can save the Earth. But all of us together, each doing his or her part, can. We can make the Earth a better place to live. We can heal its wounds, restore its health, and teach people how to live in harmony with its natural rhythms. We can recycle or reuse materials rather than throw them away. We can stop doing things that pollute the Earth's air, water, and soil. We can conserve energy and water, and we can encourage and educate others to do all of these things and more.

Often science has been blamed for the Earth's ills. Yet science can be used to help restore the Earth to health. There are thousands of ways that science and sound thinking can be applied to the Earth's problems. Carefully controlled experiments can show us how different factors affect the Earth. But science alone cannot solve the Earth's problems. People—people like you and me—must apply what we learn in practical ways to help protect the Earth. We must become conscious of how our actions affect the Earth; we must change the way we live. Only by developing a life-style based on concerns about the Earth can we ensure its well-being. We must continually ask ourselves, "How will this action affect the Earth?"

In this book, you'll find some experiments and projects that will help you begin to understand how you can improve the Earth, how you can make it a better place to live. A small book such as this one can deal with only a few of the many problems that face us. The emphasis here will be on everyday problems related to the smooth functioning of your home, school, and neighborhood: litter; solid waste and how it can be reused, recycled, or composted; air pollution; water conservation; and acid rain.

Although the topics are few, the challenges are many. Earth's future is in your hands and in those of every person living on this planet. Earth is that fragile globe that we call home. It's important that you do all you can to keep it a safe and healthy place to live and encourage others to do the same.

When we try to pick out anything
by itself, we find it hitched to
everything else in the universe.

John Muir
My First Summer in the Sierra

CHAPTER ONE

EARTH'S BIRTHDAY

*The clearest way into
the universe is through
a forest wilderness.*

John Muir
John of the Mountains

NO ONE KNOWS exactly when the Earth was born. It was probably about 5 billion years ago. Most people who study the origin of our universe think that it began about 20 billion years ago, with a huge explosion called the Big Bang. At that time, all the matter in the universe was created and flew out in all directions. Most scientists think that the universe is still flying apart.

Small parts of the newly born universe contained cloudy disks of dustlike particles. In one of these disks the particles began to pull together to form our solar system. At the center of the disk, the converging matter became very hot, and little by little our sun began to form. In the region near the sun only the heavy particles of matter, such as iron, remained solid. These solid particles slowly pulled together to form the planets closest to the sun—Mercury, Venus, Earth, and Mars. The temperature on these planets was so warm that most of the hydrogen and helium gases escaped. These gases can be found in abundance only on the large colder, outer planets—Jupiter, Saturn, Uranus, and Neptune.

In the beginning, the Earth was just a giant ball of molten rock surrounded by a dense cloud of steam. Slowly the Earth cooled, and it started to rain. The rain lasted for millions of years. As soon as the rain touched the hot ground, the water boiled away as steam.

At last, the Earth cooled enough to allow the rain to form rivers, lakes, and oceans. Of all the planets, only the Earth has the right temperature range for water to exist as a liquid. On Venus, where it's very hot, water is found only as a gas—steam. On Mars, where it's cold, water is frozen into ice. Since life seems to require liquid water, Earth was the only planet where life could exist.

By about 3.5 billion years ago, primitive forms of life began to form on Earth. About 400 million years ago animals began to slither across the land. Mammals appeared nearly 200 million years ago, but primates (monkey-like creatures) didn't appear for at least another 140 million years. The ancestors of humans were evident 2 million years ago, but people similar to us have been around for only about the last 100,000 years. Humans and their ancestors are so recent that we can't be located accurately on the depiction of the Earth's entire life span shown in Figure 1. A separate line expanding the last 2 million years had to be drawn to show where we appear in the Earth's long history. We are a very recent creature. If you think of the Earth's life span as a year, humans have been around for only the last ten minutes. If you think

Figure 1. The Development of Life on Earth

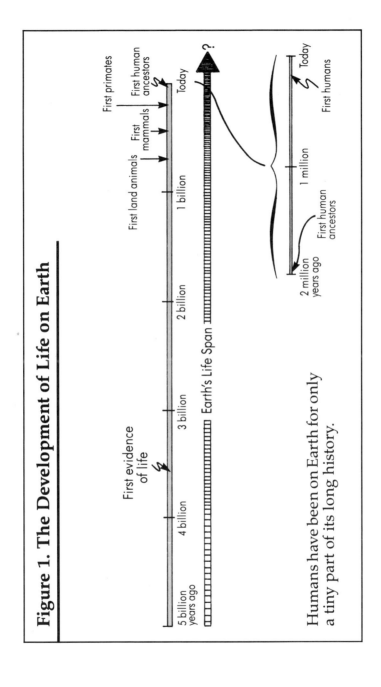

Humans have been on Earth for only a tiny part of its long history.

of it as one day, humans have been here for a little less than two seconds.

Despite our short time here, the human population has grown from a handful to billions. And our numbers are still growing, at an ever-increasing rate. Eight thousand years ago there were only about 5 million people on the Earth, and it took about 2,000 years for the population to double. By the time of the American Civil War in 1860, there were more than 1 billion people, and the population was doubling every 80 years. In the last 100 years, the human population has swelled from about 1.5 billion to more than 5 billion. The Earth's population is now increasing at a rate of a little more than 2 percent each year. As a result, the world's population is doubling about every 30 years. Project 1 will help you to understand what will happen to the population during the next two centuries if the present rate of increase continues.

Project 1:
The Earth's Ever-Growing
Number of People

In 1990, the Earth's population reached 5 billion (5,000,000,000) people. If the present rate of population growth continues, the world's population can be expected to reach 10 billion by 2020. By 2050, it will be 20 billion. The following chart shows the Earth's population growth over the next two centuries based on the present rate of growth:

Year	Population (in billions)	Year	Population (in billions)
1990	5	2110	80
2020	10	2140	160
2050	20	2170	320
2080	40	2200	640

Using food coloring and water, prepare about half a gallon of colored water. Then find eight identical quart or liter containers. (Clear plastic soda bottles would be satisfactory.) To the first container, add 5 milliliters (mL), or about 100 drops (1/6 ounce), of the colored water. The 5 mL of water represent the Earth's human population in 1990. Now, pour 10 mL of water into the second container. This volume of water represents the Earth's estimated population in 2020. Into the next jar pour 20 mL of water. What world population and year is represented by this jar? Continue to do this for each of the populations shown on the chart.

By looking at the jars placed in a row you can see how the Earth's population may grow over 30-year intervals during the next two centuries. Many believe that the Earth cannot support more than 10 billion people. If this is true, when will the Earth's population stop growing? Others claim the Earth can provide food for 30 billion people. Do you think the Earth's population will stop growing within your lifetime?

Project 2:
Population Estimates Based on Calculation

You may wonder how anyone can predict that the world's population will double in 30 years. This is an estimate, of course. We don't know exactly how fast the population is increasing. However, using census figures from all over the world, experts have been able to calculate that the population appears to be growing at a rate of between 2 and 3 percent each year. If the growth rate were exactly 2 percent each year, it would take 35 years for Earth's population to double.

Population growth is just like the interest on money in a bank. A dollar ($1.00) invested at 2 percent (0.02) yearly interest will be worth $1.02 (a dollar and two cents) one year later, since $1.00 × 1.02 = $1.02. After two years, it would grow to $1.02 × 1.02, or $1.04 (when rounded off to 3 figures). A year later it would grow to $1.04 × 1.02 = $1.06.

With a pocket calculator, keep multiplying successive values by 1.02, as shown in the method described above, until you reach $2.00. At that point, your dollar has doubled. You'll find you have to multiply (by 1.02) 35 times to reach $2.00 (actually 1.999 rounded to 2.00). Since population figures work the same way, it would take 35 years for the Earth's human population to double if the growth rate were 2 percent a year.

If the world population were growing at 3 percent (times 1.03 each year), how long would it take for the Earth's population to double? Use your calculator to find out.

It now takes about 30 years for the Earth's population to double. At about what rate do you estimate the Earth's population is growing each year? Use a calculator to check your estimate.

In 1800, the Earth's population was about 1 billion. It didn't reach 2 billion until about 1920. At what average rate was the world's population growing during those years? Was its growth less than 1 percent a year?

EFFECTS OF A GROWING POPULATION

The rapid growth of Earth's population over the last 150 years has been accompanied by an even greater demand for energy. To fuel the industrial and technological world that has developed during that time, we have been using vast amounts of fossil fuels—coal, oil, and natural gas. These fuels were formed from decaying plants and animals over millions of years, but we've been using them much faster than they were formed. The carbon dioxide gas released when these fuels burn adds to that already in the atmosphere. This increase in carbon dioxide reduces the rate at which heat can escape and threatens to make the Earth warmer, a result known as the *greenhouse effect*.

Scientists say that a warmer Earth will lead to a rise in sea level. Melting ice will increase the volume of ocean water, which may flood many present-day coastal cities. Will this rise in the oceans result from the melting of the ice that now floats freely in the Earth's seas, from the glaciers that cover arctic and antarctic lands, or from both? The next experiment will help you answer this question.

THINK ABOUT IT. What are some other consequences of a rapidly growing world population? What can be done to stop or reduce the growth rate of the Earth's population? How do religious and social issues affect people's views about the Earth and its growing population?

Experiment 1:
The Water for Rising Oceans

Place a large ice cube in a glass half-filled with water. Mark the water level on the glass with a marking pen or tape, as shown in Figure 2. Place a second ice cube in a funnel above another glass half-filled with water. Mark the water level in this glass as well.

After both ice cubes have melted, look at the water levels again. Now try to answer this question: Will the rising oceans of a warming Earth be caused by melting glaciers, by floating ice melting in the seas, or by both?

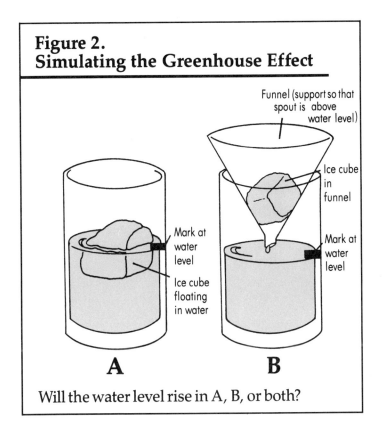

Figure 2.
Simulating the Greenhouse Effect

Funnel (support so that spout is above water level)

Ice cube in funnel

Mark at water level

Ice cube floating in water

Mark at water level

A   **B**

Will the water level rise in A, B, or both?

EARTH UNDER STRESS

The gases and particles produced when fossil fuels and their derivatives, such as gasoline, are burned pollute the Earth's atmosphere. The Earth's land and water are being polluted as well, due to a throwaway attitude. Instead of repairing and reusing machines, clothing, and furniture, we throw them away and buy new ones. Rather than recycling, reusing, or finding other uses for bottles, containers, and other materials, we are throwing them away. Much of the material we buy, such as certain plastics, cannot be used again the way glass can, nor does it decay the way paper would. Rather than put our garbage and waste back into the soil as fertilizer, we throw or flush it away.

As a result, we throw vast amounts of trash and garbage into gigantic landfills. We cover it up with dirt and try to pretend that it's no longer there. We flush away human waste and chemicals, which pollute rivers, lakes, and oceans. Water is becoming ever more scarce. Human actions place Earth's natural cycles under great stress.

Fortunately, the Earth can adjust to stress. It has ways of recycling much of the waste that we throw onto it and into it. In the chapters that follow, we'll examine some of the ways that the Earth recycles materials. But the Earth has its limits. There are limits to the amount of material it can naturally recycle. And there are some materials that it cannot recycle. We must be careful not to exceed its limits.

Population, when unchecked, increases
in a geometrical ratio. Subsistence
increases only in an arithmetical ratio.

Thomas Robert Malthus
An Essay on the
Principle of Population

CHAPTER TWO

DOWN IN THE DUMPS

The soil exists in a state of constant change, taking part in cycles that have no beginning and no end.

Rachel Carson
Silent Spring

A CENTURY AGO, food wastes (garbage) in rural areas were fed to pigs or buried in the garden. Paper was used to start fires in the kitchen stove, and plastic was unknown. In coastal cities, garbage and trash were dumped in the ocean. In other cities it was hauled to open, foul-smelling, vermin-infested dumps that were a threat to community health. To reduce this threat, many cities in the 1920s began to "modernize" their waste treatment. They built incinerators to burn garbage and trash. But the smoke, pollution, and smell from this process was even worse, so they started developing landfills. In a landfill, waste is dumped and spread out over a layer of gravel, sand, or other fill. It is then covered by another layer of fill. (See Figure 3.) Covering the garbage and trash isolates it from vermin and prevents the escape of gases that used to carry the odors of decaying waste to people who lived near open dumps.

Early landfills were often located in swamps and marshes, far away from houses. These filled-in areas later became sites for parks, athletic fields, and housing. However, the water in many of these

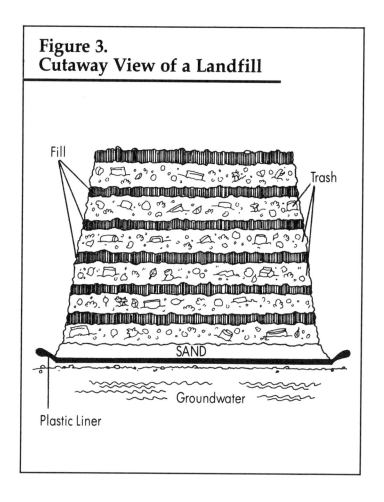

Figure 3.
Cutaway View of a Landfill

Fill

Trash

SAND

Groundwater

Plastic Liner

areas became contaminated by leachate—the liquid that percolates slowly through the landfill and may enter the groundwater, or aquifer. Modern landfills have a clay or plastic liner to trap the leachate, but 80 percent of our landfills will be filled to capacity within 20 years.

One way to reduce the problems associated with landfills is to reduce the amount of material we bury in them. Figure 4 shows the percentage of each type of solid waste generated in the United States. Since each of the country's 250 million people produces about 4 pounds (1.8 kg) of solid waste per day, we, as a nation, generate a billion pounds per day, or 365 billion pounds (about 180 million tons) per year. Even if it were all compacted in a landfill, this waste would still occupy more than 7 billion cubic feet—enough to cover the entire city of Washington, D.C., with a layer of trash 4 feet (1.2 m) deep.

To reduce the amount of material buried in landfills, we need to recycle, reuse, compost, and reduce the sources of solid waste. Many articles can be easily repaired and used again. Glass, cans, and some paper and plastic can be recycled. Many state legislatures have passed "bottle bills" that require stores to ask for a deposit on each can or bottle of beverage purchased. When you return the can or bottle, you get back the deposit.

Today, about 60 percent of all aluminum cans are recycled. Every can that is recycled saves the energy needed to mine and process bauxite, the primary source of aluminum. Similarly, glass bottles can be reused or broken into small pieces (cullet) that can be melted to make new bottles or

Figure 4.
Solid Waste in the Average Household

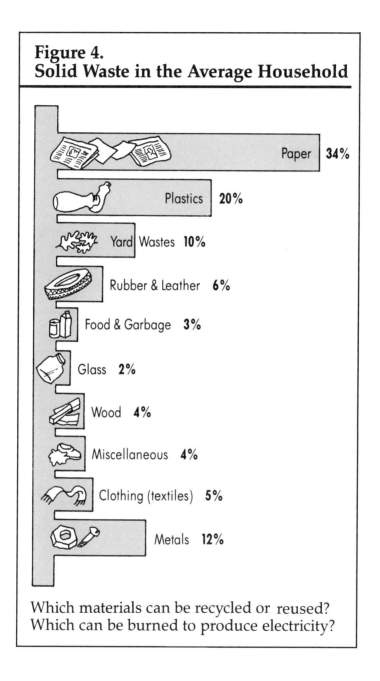

Paper **34%**

Plastics **20%**

Yard Wastes **10%**

Rubber & Leather **6%**

Food & Garbage **3%**

Glass **2%**

Wood **4%**

Miscellaneous **4%**

Clothing (textiles) **5%**

Metals **12%**

Which materials can be recycled or reused?
Which can be burned to produce electricity?

fiberglass insulation. Paper, too, can be recycled to produce stationery, towels, bags, wrapping, and newspapers.

In April 1991, McDonald's announced a plan to use more recycled materials and to cut its trash by 80 percent in an effort to reduce the amount of waste it sends to landfills. It had already begun by wrapping hamburgers in paper instead of putting them in plastic sandwich boxes. Then the company took another step. It started to use brown bags made from recycled paper in place of white paper. The white paper was made white by bleaching with chlorine, which produces toxic by-products. Reusable coffee mugs are now being purchased to replace the throwaway plastic cups. Plans are also under way to replace plastic cutlery with starch-based, biodegradable material. Behind the counter, pump-style bulk dispensers for condiments will eventually replace the small plastic-covered packets. Cardboard cartons will be recycled, and new, reusable coffee filters will be introduced.

Even with the changes, McDonald's outlets will send 200 tons of trash each day to incinerators and landfills across the country. But this will be far better than the 1,000 tons of trash now being generated daily at McDonald's restaurants across the country. Furthermore, their decision to use recycled paper may help to increase the demand for waste paper, much of which is now buried in landfills.

Experiment 2:
Recycling Paper

Paper can be recycled and used in place of wood fibers to make new paper. In this experiment you'll make paper with and without cornstarch to see what effect it has on the quality of the paper produced.

Cut a single sheet of a newspaper into small pieces about half an inch (1.25 cm) square. *Ask a parent or another adult for help* in using a blender that can pulverize the paper. Place one cup of hot water in the blender. Then pour the paper into the blender. Mix 3 tablespoons of cornstarch with another cup of hot water and add the mixture to the blender. *Ask the parent or other adult* to plug in the blender and turn it on. Swirl and chop the mixture of paper and water until it has the consistency of a thin, gray "gravy."

Next, pour about 1 inch (2.5 cm) of water into a large pan that is about 12 inches (30 cm) on a side and 3 inches (7.5 cm) deep. Then place a piece of stiff window screening in the pan. (If you have only a soft, flexible screen, build a small wooden frame and use thumbtacks to stretch the screen across the opening in the frame and place it in the pan. Be sure the screen is covered with water.) Now pour one cup of the pulverized paper and water mixture over the screen. Use your fingers to spread the gray goo evenly over the screen. Then lift the screen and let the excess water drain back into the pan.

Place an opened newspaper several sheets thick on a table or floor. Place the pulp-covered screen on the newspaper. Close the newspaper and carefully turn it over so that the screen is now on top of the pulverized paper. Use a rolling pin to squeeze water from the pulp. The newspaper above and below the pulp will absorb the water. Open the newspaper and leave the pulp untouched until it is thoroughly dry. Then peel the paper you have made from the newspaper and screen. If the paper is very thick, you've made cardboard.

Can you write on the paper? How is the paper different from the paper you normally write on? Why do you think it's different?

Repeat the experiment, but this time do not add cornstarch to the second cup of hot water. Do you see any difference between paper made with and without starch?

DUMPS AND DECOMPOSITION

Landfill developers assumed that the materials dumped in landfills would decompose into soil in a few years, just as dead leaves, wood, and grass do in forests and fields. But during the late 1970s, archaeologists at the University of Arizona made a startling discovery. Upon digging into landfills, they found twenty-five-year-old newspapers and magazines that were still readable, undecayed leaves from yard waste, and even food items that could be identified, such as mummified hot dogs. Although these materials are biodegradable, they did not decompose as expected, due to the absence of air and moisture in many landfills.

Today, researchers are looking for better ways to design landfills. By adding bacteria and moisture, they hope to make buried wastes rot faster. Others are trying to find ways to entomb waste permanently in dry, sealed landfills so that leachate and gases cannot escape.

Experiment 3:
The Dos and Don'ts
of Decomposition

Many materials are biodegradable. That means they will decompose and eventually become part of nature's soil and air. To find out which substances will decompose and which won't, you'll need to bury some samples in soil when the weather is warm. You might test food waste, such as a lettuce leaf, an apple core, or potato peels; yard waste, such as grass clippings or shredded weeds or leaves; cloth from natural sources, such as cotton or wool; synthetic cloth, such as nylon; a plastic bag or pieces of Styrofoam; aluminum foil; and paper—both recycled and new. If you have a yard, use a small spade to dig a hole a few inches (10–20 cm) deep for each sample. Place the sample in the hole and cover it up with the dirt you removed. Place a coffee stirrer or Popsicle stick in the center of the covered hole. The stick should be labeled (use a waterproof pen or pencil) with a name or number so you can later identify the buried material. Do this for each sample. If the soil becomes dry, water it from time to time.

After a month, dig up each sample. Which ones show evidence of decomposition? Which ones seem not to have decomposed at all? Cover up the samples once more and check them again after another month or so. Continue to do this for as long as possible. Are there some substances that still show no signs of decomposition after many months in the soil?

If you don't have a yard where you can bury things, put the samples in some soil from outdoors (not potting soil) in separate plastic containers such as large margarine tubs. Label the containers so you'll know where each sample is buried. Cover each sample with soil, and put them in a warm place. Keep the soil damp, not wet, by adding water occasionally.

COLLECTING AND SEPARATING CANS

Many communities recycle metal. In states that have bottle laws, stores will pay a small amount, usually 5 cents, for each can or bottle you return. If you live in such a state, you have an opportunity to make money and improve the environment at the same time. Often, you will be able to find empty cans left by people who didn't return them to a store. You can pick up the cans, which will make the environment look better, and return them to a store, where they will be sent away for recycling. At the same time, you can make 5 cents for every can you return.

Experiment 4:
Separating Cans for Recycling

If your community recycles cans, it may want them separated according to the metals they contain. Most cans are made of aluminum or steel. Tin cans are made of steel but have a thin coating of tin over the steel. The tin prevents the food inside from acquiring a metallic taste. How can you tell an aluminum can from a tin (steel) can or a can that has both aluminum and steel? Generally, steel cans have a seam; aluminum cans don't. Steel cans feel heavier than aluminum cans of the same size. But here's a sure way to tell: Hold a magnet on a can that you know is made of aluminum. Now hold the magnet on a tin can. To which can is the magnet attracted?

How could you use a magnet to identify steel cans with aluminum tops? Can you find any cans that are made partly of aluminum and partly of steel?

Project 3:
A Recycling Activity for Earth Day

Have a contest to see which school, grade, or classroom can collect the greatest number of recyclable cans and bottles by Earth Day. Ask your teacher or principal to help you organize it. In states that have a bottle law, the winner can collect the money for the returnables and decide how it should be spent to make the Earth a better place. It might be used to buy trees or flowers, trash containers, or whatever the winner thinks would be most appropriate.

Experiment 5:
Separating Trash

At many landfills or incinerators where solid waste is burned to produce electric power, the trash must be separated. Metals such as aluminum and steel are separated for recycling. Glass is also usually recycled, but paper and plastics may be recycled or burned. This experiment, which should be done on a dry day when there is very little humidity, will help you to see how this might be done, at least on a small scale.

Place on a table or countertop several paper clips, rubber bands, and small steel washers; some small pieces of aluminum foil, paper towel, and toothpicks; a couple of marbles and pennies; and a small plastic straw cut into small pieces. Mix all the materials together.

Now that you have gathered all this trash into one place, you're ready to begin separating it. Start by moving a strong magnet over your pile of trash. Which material is removed by the magnet? Next blow up a rubber balloon. Give the balloon a static electric charge by rubbing it against your hair or woolen clothing. Move the balloon over the trash pile. Which materials are attracted by the balloon's electric charge?

Dump any trash that remains into a pan of water. Which materials float? Which ones sink? How would you separate the "floaters" from one another? The "sinkers"?

THINK ABOUT IT. There are many problems involved in recycling glass, metal, and especially paper, plastics, and old tires, which tend to rise and "pop" out of landfills. Investigate and think about these problems. Read books and articles related to recycling in your school or public library. Talk to and ask for information from local officials involved in recycling, paper companies, glass factories, bottling plants, and other people or organizations that may have useful information.

If paper, plastic, and other trash is burned to produce electric power, what should be done with the ashes that remain? Are the gases and particles produced when trash burns harmful? If so, what can be done about them?

Would recycling problems be reduced if recycling was required nationwide? How?

Project 4:
Giving Throwaways a Second Life

Many of the items we send to landfills might be repaired or used for something else. For example, a sock with a hole in it could be mended. An old shower curtain may be too shabby for the bathroom, but it could still be used as a drop cloth when a room needs painting. A plastic margarine tub and cover might make an excellent container for leftovers that you wish to place in a freezer.

Organize a group to brainstorm second uses for articles that are commonly discarded. You could have a swap box in each classroom where kids could put things they no longer want. Some kind of raffle system could be established to decide who gets items for which there is great demand. Don't forget thrift shops, schools, libraries, day-care centers, shelters for the homeless, and other such places. They can often make good use of articles that you want to get rid of.

WASTE TO SOIL: DECOMPOSITION

Bacteria and fungi normally found in soil convert organic matter (such as food wastes, grass clippings, leaves, and dead wood) to humus. Humus is the black matter found in topsoil. It is formed as leaves and grass in forests, meadows, and plains are gradually decomposed by bacteria and fungi into nutrients that can be absorbed by plants. The plants use these nutrients to grow new leaves, stems, and roots. To find out what is needed for these bacteria and fungi to do their work, you can use a common fungus—bread mold.

Experiment 6:
The Essentials of Decomposition

Take three slices of bread to which *no* mold inhibitor has been added and gently tear the slices in half. (If a mold inhibitor, such as sodium propionate, has been added to the bread, it will appear on the label.) Place each half-slice in a plastic container that has a cover. One container should be transparent or semitransparent, so that light can reach the bread. Put a few drops of water in five of the containers to be sure the bread stays moist. The bread that is to go into the sixth container should first be placed in a warm, not hot, oven until it is dry. Then place it in its container and add the cover. Check the containers daily to be sure that all but the dry one have a few drops of moisture.

The most common molds found on bread will be white, black, or green in color. When mold begins to form on one or more slices, use a pin or a toothpick to transfer some of the mold to each piece of bread. If more than one type of mold appears, transfer a little of each kind to each piece of bread.

Once mold has been placed on all the bread, you can separate the bread as shown in Figure 5. Place one container in a freezer, another in a refrigerator, and a third in a warm, dark place. The container that allows light to enter should be placed in a warm place where it will receive bright

Figure 5. Growing Mold in Bread

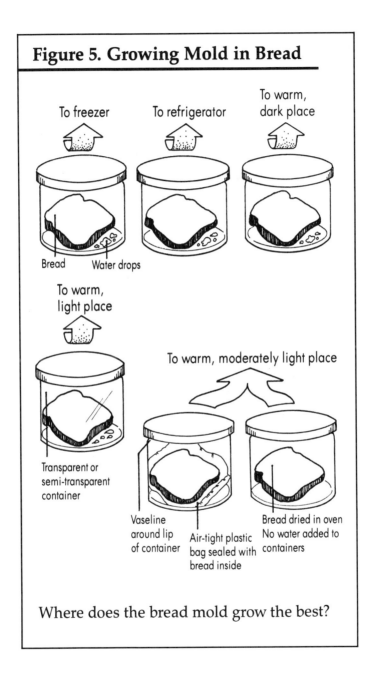

Where does the bread mold grow the best?

light. The fifth container will be used to keep the bread in an airtight environment. To do this, place the moldy bread in a zip-lock plastic bag. Flatten the bag as much as possible to remove air from around the bread. Then seal the bag and put it in the container. To further ensure that fresh air does not reach the bread, spread petroleum jelly around the lip of the container. This will make an airtight seal when the lid is placed on. Turn the lid back and forth a few times to spread the sealant evenly. The dry bread should remain in the sixth container.

After a week, *put on rubber or plastic gloves* and open each container. *Avoid breathing any spores that may be in the containers.* Compare the growths in the containers. Do molds need warm temperatures to grow? Do they need moisture? Do they need air? Will they grow where it is cool? Where it is freezing? Do they need light? Compare the mold growth on the side of the bread exposed to light with that on the other side, which was shaded by the bread itself.

If more than one type of mold was growing on your bread samples, you may be able to compare the growth in the different containers. Do some molds grow better under certain conditions than others? Under what conditions do none of the molds seem to grow?

After you've finished, be sure to put the moldy bread in the garbage or on your compost pile. (See Project 5.) The containers can then be thoroughly washed in warm, soapy water.

Experiment 7:
Something to Do With
a Halloween Pumpkin

When Halloween is over, ask an adult to help you cut a jack-o'-lantern in half. Put half the pumpkin in a warm oven until it is thoroughly dry. Then keep it in your house on a newspaper. Put the other half of the pumpkin outside. Put both pumpkin halves in places where they won't be disturbed.

On which pumpkin half do you expect to see mold? Why don't you expect to see mold on the other half? Which pumpkin half will decompose first? How long do you think it will take?

COMPOSTING AND DECOMPOSITION

Organic (living or once-living) materials will decompose naturally, given moisture, air, and warmth —and provided that the bacteria and fungi normally found in soils are present. In fact they will decompose, although more slowly, even without air. Some of the bacteria and fungi that decompose organic matter are anaerobic; they do not need oxygen to live and can digest plant and animal remains in the absence of air. In addition to moisture and warmth these microorganisms need carbon as an energy source and nitrogen as a protein source to build their own bodies. They can get the carbon from tough plant matter such as straw, leaves, and sawdust. Grass clippings, humus, or green vegetables in garbage can provide the nitrogen.

Composting is simply a way of increasing the natural rate at which organic matter decomposes. Many landfills now compost yard wastes and garbage to reduce the volume of material going into the landfill. The humus (compost) produced by decomposition can then be sold or given away. The compost provides a rich soil or mulch for gardens and flower beds.

You can make your own compost at home. The next project suggests some ways of composting materials that might otherwise be sent to a landfill.

Project 5:
Composting Organic Waste

Since the beginning of agriculture, farmers have spread manure on their soil, buried garbage in their gardens, and plowed "green manure" crops such as rye grass back into the earth. These materials then decompose, providing new soil and nourishment for plants.

In this project, you can choose one or more of the composting methods suggested here. What you choose to do will depend on where you live and what organic materials you normally throw away.

Composting Garbage · Place a 32-gallon (120-L) plastic trash container on four or five bricks in your backyard. The container should have 3/8-inch (1-cm) holes about 2 inches (5 cm) apart in its sides and bottom. *Ask an adult* to drill these holes for you. Cover the bottom of the container with pine needles or green twigs. This will allow air to reach the waste material that will be in the bottom of the container.

Collect your food wastes—except for fatty materials, meat, and bones—in a 1-gallon (4.5-L) covered, plastic container beneath the sink. Do not include cat litter or any matter that is not biodegradable. Tear or cut the waste into small pieces before placing it in the container. *You might even ask an adult to chop the material in a blender.* When the container is full, empty it into the large trash container you have prepared. Sprinkle a layer of pine needles, grass clippings, or chopped leaves on the garbage each time you add waste to the large container. Then secure the cover to the container with an elastic cord.

While you are gradually filling the large container, prepare a second one just like the first. Again, *ask an adult* to drill the holes in the sides and bottom. Place the second large container beside the first one. When the first container is full, use a shovel or garden fork to transfer the waste from the first container into the second. The last waste added will then be on the bottom of the new container and the oldest waste on the top. Don't be alarmed by insects or worms in the waste. They help to decompose and mix the waste.

By the time you have filled the first container again, the waste in the second container may be ready for your garden or flower beds. If it is "done," it will be cool, dark, and crumbly. It should smell earthy, not moldy or rotten. If it's not ready, transfer it to a third container identical to the first two. If it appears to be well decomposed, wheel it to your garden, dump it, and mix it with the garden soil.

Although it will take longer to decompose completely, you can simply bury food wastes about 8 inches (20 cm) below the surface of your garden. Dig up the buried waste after several months to see how rapidly it is rotting. Be sure to bury it again when you have finished.

A Large, Mixed Compost Pile · Build a container like the one shown in Figure 6 to hold your compost. The wire allows air to reach the decaying matter. The hooks and eyes make it easy to move the compost pile; the fence can be taken apart and reassembled quickly. The larger size will cause the pile to heat up more quickly and thus speed up the rate of decay.

Start with about 6 inches (15 cm) of organic material (kitchen waste, weeds, dead flowers, or vegetable leaves—but no fats, meat, or bones). Add a 2-inch (5-cm) layer of rich soil. Then sprinkle on a handful of powdered limestone before repeating the layering process with another layer of organic matter.

If you have enough matter to build immediately a pile 3 feet (1 m) high, you may have finished compost in a couple of months. But if you build your pile gradually, it will take longer—a year or more— to develop compost ready for gardens. This is because a compost pile that grows slowly will not become warm enough to speed the growth and

Figure 6. Making Compost Bins

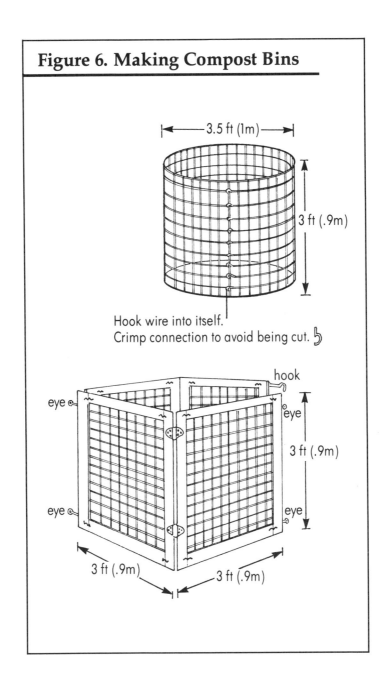

|← 3.5 ft (1m) →|

3 ft (.9m)

Hook wire into itself.
Crimp connection to avoid being cut.

hook

eye

eye

eye

eye

3 ft (.9m)

3 ft (.9m)

3 ft (.9m)

47

activity of the microorganisms that bring about decomposition.

Add water, if necessary, to keep the compost damp but not wet. It should feel like a damp sponge from which the water has been squeezed. It may be necessary to poke holes so that moisture and air can reach the inner parts of the pile.

When the original materials have changed in color and consistency, turn the pile over. This is easily done by unhooking the wire fence and moving it so it is next to the pile. Then use a shovel or pitchfork to move the compost pile to its new location. The recently added matter will now be on the bottom of the pile and the original matter will be on top.

Slower-Acting Compost Piles · Compost piles that decompose more slowly can be made by alternating layers of chopped leaves or straw with layers of humus, manure, or garbage, and thin layers of sawdust or shredded paper. Dustings of 10-5-10 fertilizer and limestone may help the pile to decay. The addition of composting bacteria, which can be purchased at a garden center, will help, too.

The idea is to mix materials rich in carbon (such as leaves, straw, paper, and sawdust) with materials that contain a lot of nitrogen (such as humus, manure, grass, and food wastes).

A Worm Box · Earthworms eat and digest organic matter by passing it along their digestive tract, which includes a gizzard where food is ground by tiny stones. The earthworms excrete dark, fertile, granular castings rich in nutrients that plants can use. You can buy composting earthworms from a garden-supply company. Calculate the average weight of garbage you produce per day. You'll need to order twice this weight in earthworms.

Before the worms arrive, find a wooden box about 2 feet (60 cm) on a side. Fill it with moist, shredded newspapers and put it in a place where it will not freeze or become very warm. The newspaper will serve as bedding for the worms. Put the worms in the box and feed them your garbage, except for animal products. If possible, *have an adult grind the garbage in a blender* before adding it to the worm box.

Every couple of months, move the worms and bedding to one side of the box and put fresh, moist, shredded paper in the other side. Begin putting your garbage on the fresh bedding. After the worms migrate to the new bedding, remove the castings from the old bedding. The castings can be spread on the soil of potted plants or flower beds or used as soil for seedlings.

Experiment 8:
Factors That Affect Composting

You can test the effects of different materials on decomposition by varying the materials you put together in miniature compost piles. You'll need five large plastic tubs, each about the size of a fish tank (aquarium). Each tub will contain alternate layers of soil (1 inch, or 2.5 cm, deep), organic waste (2 inches, or 5 cm), a sprinkling of 10-5-10 fertilizer, and enough water to dampen the pile throughout. Repeat this layering until the tub is filled. In one container, use food wastes (but no fat, bones, or meat) as the organic layer. In a second, use chopped leaves as the organic layer. *Ask an adult to use a blender or food processor* to chop the leaves into small pieces. In a third, use grass clippings for the organic layer. In a fourth, use food wastes again, but this time *ask an adult to use a blender or food processor* to chop the food into small pieces. In a fifth, use chopped leaves again as the organic material, and add a few earthworms to the container. Keep all the tubs in a warm place.

Because these miniature compost piles are so small, their temperatures will not rise as high as those that have a volume of a cubic yard or more. Nevertheless, you can use a thermometer to measure the temperature at the center of each pile every day. Which tub gets warmest? After the temperature in a tub reaches a peak and starts to fall, use a small garden tool to mix the compost. This will allow more air to reach the decaying matter. Add water, when necessary, to keep the material as damp as a squeezed sponge.

Which organic matter decays into soil faster: food wastes, leaves, or grass clippings? How does chopping the matter into small pieces affect the rate of decay within the pile? What effects do earthworms have on the decay process? What can you do with the material in the tubs after all the miniature compost piles have turned to soil?

THINK ABOUT IT. Composting is a great way to reduce the volume of materials sent to landfills and to transform wastes into soil. Building a compost pile is not difficult if you live in the country or suburbs, but what about people who live in cities? What can be done so that people who live in cities can compost their kitchen wastes?

A land ethic for tomorrow should . . . stress the oneness of our resources and the live-and-help-live logic of the great chain of life. If in our haste to 'progress,' the economics of ecology are disregarded by citizens and policy makers alike, the result will be an ugly America.

Stewart Udall
The Quiet Crisis

CHAPTER THREE

LET'S LITTER LESS

*The long fight to save wild
beauty represents democracy
at its best. It requires citizens
to practice the hardest of all
virtues—self-restraint.*

Edwin Way Teale
Circle of the Seasons

LITTER TOSSED AWAY by thoughtless people not only mars the Earth's appearance but can be dangerous as well. A discarded bottle may break and cause serious cuts if someone accidentally steps on it. Empty cans and other containers can trap small animals, and larger animals may get their heads caught in them. Plastic six-pack rings have frequently been found around the necks of small animals and often become "choke collars" for birds that poke their heads through them. Whenever you remove a six-pack ring from beverage cans, be sure to cut each ring so that it can never encircle an animal's neck or limbs.

OCEAN LITTER

Dumping plastic material into the ocean is particularly dangerous. A decade ago, about 7 million tons of plastic were dumped into the ocean each year. There are two serious problems with this. The plastic floats, and (unlike garbage) it does not decompose. Many seabirds eat small pieces of plastic, mistaking them for fish eggs. Sea turtles often gobble up plastic bags, which look like jelly-fish to them. One beached whale was found to have fifty plastic bags in its stomach. The plastic materials may block the animals' intestines, causing them to die from starvation. Turtles, birds, seals, and even whales become entangled by plastic fishing nets that have been abandoned. Fishing nets may also wrap around ship propellers, and other plastic articles may cover the water intake of a ship's motor, possibly damaging the ship.

As a result of the effects of plastic articles and netting on birds, fish, mammals, and ships, it is now illegal to dump plastic trash into the ocean or other navigable waters. That's why you see signs reading STOW IT DON'T THROW IT on many ships. Should you see a ship dumping plastic overboard, record the name of the ship and its position, and the nature of the material discarded. If possible, take photographs to confirm your report to the harbormaster of the nearest port. If a conviction follows, you will be paid part of the fine.

David Manski, of the Cape Cod National Seashore, is conducting a five-year study of the trash that washes up on the beaches of Cape Cod. In 1990, he found more than 27,000 pieces on 5 half-mile (800-m) sections. The next project will allow you to see some of the same things Manski found.

Project 6:
Beachcombing for Litter

If you live near or have occasion to visit an ocean beach, spend some time picking up the litter along the shore. You'll need a garbage bag for the litter, *disposable rubber gloves* to protect your hands, and a notepad and pencil to keep a record of the things you find. (Even with rubber gloves, watch for sharp objects.) How many different items did you find? How many were made of plastic? Where do you think these articles came from? Which items do you think came from the ocean? Which do you think were left on the beach by careless sunbathers or swimmers? What could you do to find out?

From your investigation, can you see why it is important to recycle, incinerate, or eliminate plastics rather than throw them away?

If you live near the ocean, you will probably be able to find local organizations that help keep the beaches clean. Join such an organization, and do your part. If there are no such organizations, talk to a local official about forming a group. Now that the dumping of plastic into the ocean is forbidden, the amount of trash washing up on beaches should gradually decline. However, it will probably take a century to remove the vast amounts of trash that are already in the oceans. But it's a task worth doing, and it's one in which almost anyone can help.

Project 7:
Combing for Litter in Your
Neighborhood or School Yard

You can improve the appearance of your neighborhood or school yard by organizing groups to pick up litter. Have one person in each group carry a garbage bag while two or three others, *wearing rubber gloves,* pick up the litter and put it in the bag or bags. *Have an adult* (wearing rubber gloves) present to pick up dangerous materials such as broken glass or disposable syringes. *Place such materials in a separate bag.*

Once the area is free of litter you may want to sort and separate the collected litter to meet the requirements of your local landfill or to determine the major source of litter. Separate the litter into glass, paper, plastic, metal cans (aluminum and steel), other metal, yard waste, food waste, and any other categories that are needed. Record and count each type of litter. You might like to make a bar graph or a pie graph from your information to show what fraction of the trash you found was glass, paper, metal, and so forth. The graph could be used as part of a presentation you might make to your class, landfill director, or local officials.

Take the litter you have collected and sorted to your local landfill. Ask the landfill director how the percentages of different types of litter that you've collected compare with what is normally brought to the landfill. Which kinds of litter can be recycled? Which can be burned to generate electricity? Which can be composted? Which must be placed in the landfill and covered?

Have the groups involved in the cleanup discuss the findings. Can they explain where the various types of litter came from? If not, can a survey be made to discover the sources of litter? Discuss what can be done to reduce or eliminate the litter in the area that you cleaned up. Don't underestimate what you have done. Your example may be contagious and make those who thoughtlessly litter more conscious of their actions.

THINK ABOUT IT. How can you use litter, trash, and other throwaway items for art and craft projects? If you think about it, you can probably find ways to use litter for making sculptures, dolls, collages, and other art forms.

Project 8:
Celebrate the New Year by Chipping Christmas Trees

At the start of each new year, landfills are swamped by discarded Christmas trees. See if you can get a local tree nursery or landscaper to volunteer a wood chipper to chip these trees into a pine-fragrant mulch. Many people will be happy to take some of the mulch for their gardens. The rest could be sold or given to the landscaper or tree nursery.

An even better solution is to get people to buy live trees and plant them after Christmas. This approach not only reduces the volume of landfill waste, it increases the number of trees and helps to reduce the greenhouse effect.

Experiment 9:
How Much Waste Do You Generate?

Collect all the waste—garbage, paper, metal, plastic, etc.—that your family discards in one week. To weigh all this waste, first find out how much you weigh by standing on a scale. Weigh yourself again while holding a bag of trash. How much do you and the bag of trash weigh? How much does the trash weigh? Do this for each bag of trash that has been generated during the week. What is the total weight of all the trash? Assume that all members of the family are equally responsible for the trash. Divide the total weight of the trash by the number of people in your family. How much trash did *you* generate in one week?

Repeat the experiment for your classroom at school. How much waste did your class throw away? Assuming all students produce the same amount of waste, how much did *you* throw away? What is the *total* weight of the waste you threw away in one week (at home and at school)? From your measurements, estimate the total waste you discard in one year. Estimate the total waste generated by your family in one year.

Which of the materials discarded by either family members or classmates could be recycled? Which of them *should* have been recycled? Could any of the material have been reused or repaired?

THINK ABOUT IT. Many people who litter are not conscious of what they are doing. Because of poor habits, they act without thinking. You may find such mindless behavior among your own family and friends. What can you do to make such people aware of their behavior in an informative and friendly way? What can be done to break their bad habits?

Experiment 10:
Why Should We Crush or
Break Down Trash?

Landfills often request that cans or boxes and other forms of trash be crushed or broken down. Does crushing reduce the weight of the material? To find out, weigh a metal can on a balance. Step on the can to crush it; now reweigh it. Does it weigh less when crushed? If not, why do some landfills request that some materials be crushed or broken down?

PACKAGING: A MAJOR SOURCE OF TRASH

One way to reduce trash and litter is to eliminate their sources. It's well known that people often buy a product because of the package rather than the contents. When the package is thrown away, the volume of trash that must be transported to a landfill is increased. Packaging may account for 10 to 50 percent of the cost of a product. Some packaging is needed to protect the merchandise, but usually not all of it. Often the package is made of plastic, which is not biodegradable. Plastics account for one third of the weight that enters landfills and as much as half of the volume. We need to be more conscious of the waste that stems from packaging and more concerned about finding ways to reduce the amount of packaging we purchase and then discard.

Experiment 11:
Packaging Costs and Size

Does an 8-ounce box of cereal cost half as much as a 16-ounce box? Here's a way to see how the cost of an item is related to its packaging. At a super-market, compare the prices of different-sized packages of cereal, milk, juice, frozen vegetables, ice cream, coffee, and as many other products as possible. Use a chart like the one below to make a record of the items you price. A sample for a certain brand and kind of cereal is shown in the chart. You should record the information for the first three columns while in the store. The price per pound or per ounce can be calculated at home.

Product	Size of package	Price	Price per pound	ounce
cereal flakes	18 oz.	$4.05	$3.60	20.0¢
cereal flakes	12 oz.	$2.89	$3.85	24.0¢
cereal flakes	7 oz.	$1.89	$4.32	27.0¢

Using the information you have collected, plot a graph of price per pound or ounce versus package size for each of the products you priced. A sample graph for the cereal shown in the chart can be found in Figure 7.

As the size increases, what happens to the price per pound or ounce for each of the products you examined? What do you think accounts for this difference in cost per unit of weight or volume?

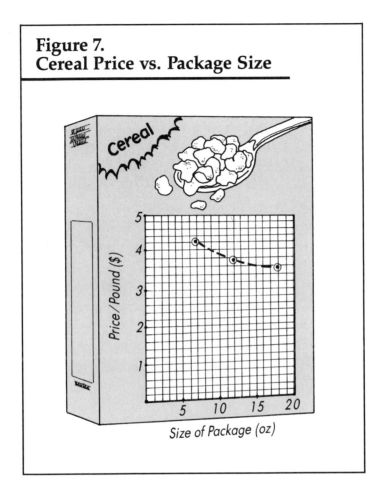

Figure 7.
Cereal Price vs. Package Size

Price/Pound ($)

Size of Package (oz)

A 9.6-ounce variety pack that contained ten individual cereal servings cost $3.59. How much did it cost per ounce? Per pound? Where would its cost per pound lie on the graph in Figure 7? Why do you think it is so much more expensive per pound?

Buy a variety pack of cereal (one that consists of ten single-serving packages) and an equal weight of cereal in a large box. As the cereals are eaten, keep all the packaging materials. When all the cereal is gone, compare the weight of the large single package of cereal with *all* the packaging that surrounded and contained the small variety cereal boxes. How do the weights compare? Then compare the surface area of the paper, plastic, and cardboard from the large single package of cereal with that from the variety pack. You can find the area (length × width) of each side, top, and bottom, and add them together to get the total area of each box. How do the total areas compare?

Processing as well as packaging adds to the price of food. Compare the prices per pound of a large bag of fresh potatoes, a large bag of potato chips, and a small individual-serving size bag of potato chips. How do you account for the differences in price per pound?

Project 9:
Finding Ways to Reduce Packaging

Organize a group interested in reducing the waste that comes with excessive packaging. Discuss with them ways in which this can be accomplished. For example, you learned in Experiment 11 that buying products in bulk will keep packaging at a minimum. People can carry groceries in their own canvas bags rather than using bags provided by supermarkets. (Many supermarkets now sell these canvas bags.) They can buy packages that can be reused or recycled. They can ask companies that use excessive packaging—some products contain three layers of packaging—to use simpler packages. Make a list of all the ways the group has suggested. Then try to figure out how to bring about the changes you'd like to see.

In those cases where the group thinks that the packaging should be simpler, design an alternative, convenient package that protects the product but requires less material. Take into account cost as well as using materials that can be recycled before submitting your design to the company that makes the product.

Use it up, wear it out,
make it do, or do without!

New England Yankee saying

CHAPTER FOUR

EARTH'S AIR AND WATER

*Of all our natural resources,
water has become the most precious.*

Rachel Carson
Silent Spring

TWO THIRDS of the Earth's surface is covered with water, and the entire Earth is blanketed by air, a mixture of primarily two gases—nitrogen (78 percent) and oxygen (21 percent). There are also small amounts of argon, carbon dioxide, water vapor (a gas), and trace quantities of other gases. The composition of the air remains remarkably constant. However, the amount of carbon dioxide in the air has been slowly increasing since the beginning of the Industrial Revolution. This is due mostly to the burning of fossil fuels—coal, oil, and natural gas—all of which contain carbon. The crude oil pumped from the Earth is sent to refineries, where it is separated into a number of components—fuel oil, gasoline, kerosene, etc.— most of which are burned to release their energy. When fossil fuels burn, they combine with oxygen to form carbon dioxide and (with the exception of coal) water vapor.

The increasing amount of carbon dioxide being pumped into the atmosphere by burning fuels is now being compounded by a decrease in the number of rain forests on Earth. These forests remove large amounts of carbon dioxide from the atmosphere by photosynthesis—a process in which green plants use the energy in sunlight to chemically unite atmospheric carbon dioxide with water, producing food.

Presently, rain forests in Central and South America are being cut at a rate of 50 acres (20 hectares) per minute to create pastures for cattle. More than 40 percent of the rain forests in Central America have been converted to pastureland— land that will be used to grow beef for North Americans, land that used to remove vast amounts of carbon dioxide from the air, land that used to supply medicinal drugs used in prescriptions.

When fossil fuels burn, tiny particles within the fuels may not burn, giving rise to soot or ash, which contaminates the air. These particles are so small that you may not be aware of them. Experiment 12 will help to convince you that they really do exist. And Experiment 13 will help you to see at least one effect of air pollution.

Experiment 12:
Capturing Particles in the Air

Find a wide, shallow plastic cup. *Ask an adult* to help you make two holes on opposite sides of the cup near the top. These can be made by holding the sharp end of a pin in a match flame, then pushing the hot pin through the plastic cup, as shown in Figure 8.

Figure 8.
Capturing Particles from the Air

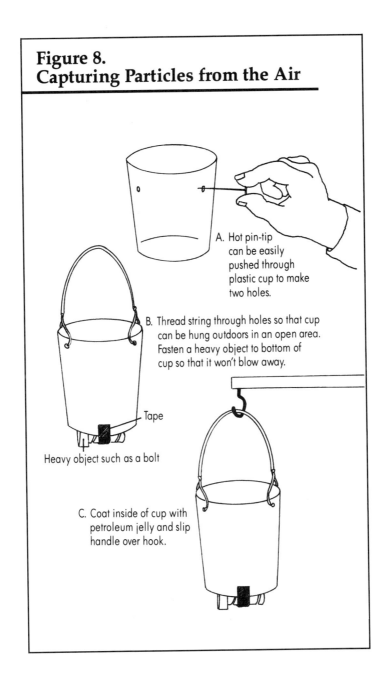

A. Hot pin-tip can be easily pushed through plastic cup to make two holes.

B. Thread string through holes so that cup can be hung outdoors in an open area. Fasten a heavy object to bottom of cup so that it won't blow away.

Tape

Heavy object such as a bolt

C. Coat inside of cup with petroleum jelly and slip handle over hook.

Thread or twine can then be used to suspend the cup in the air outside your home or school. Fasten a heavy bolt or similar object to the outside of the cup's bottom to keep the cup from blowing away. Coat the inside of the cup with a thin, smooth layer of petroleum jelly so that any particles that fall into the cup will stick to it. Be sure to hang the cup in an open area. If it starts to rain, bring the cup inside. Place it outside again after the rain has passed.

After about a week, use scissors to cut the cup carefully into several pieces. This will allow you to look more closely at any particles that are stuck to the jelly. Use a hand lens to examine the particles. Can you identify any of them?

If you have access to a microscope, coat the center region of several microscope slides with a thin, smooth layer of petroleum jelly. Place these slides in different places around your home or school. If a wood stove or fireplace is burning nearby, or if someone is burning leaves and there is a very gentle breeze, place several slides downwind from the smoke and several upwind. Leave the slides for several hours. Then cover the petroleum jelly area of each slide with a cover slip. Examine the slides with a hand lens and then with a microscope. Can you detect particles that fell from the air onto the jelly? How do the number of particles on the slides that were downwind from the smoke compare with the number on the slides that were upwind?

Experiment 13:
Rubber Bands and Air Pollution

Take two wire coat hangers and stretch several identical rubber bands onto them as shown in Figure 9. Cover one of the coat hangers with a large

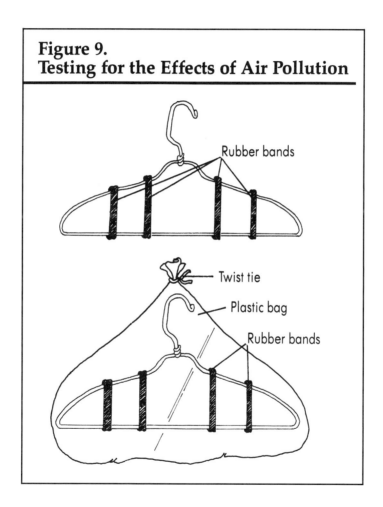

Figure 9.
Testing for the Effects of Air Pollution

Rubber bands

Twist tie

Plastic bag

Rubber bands

plastic bag and seal it. Hang both sets of rubber bands in a shady place at least several feet above the ground. After about two weeks, inspect both sets of rubber bands with a hand lens. Do you see any differences between the bands that were exposed to the air and those that were protected by the plastic bag? Stretch both sets of rubber bands by the same amount. Can you feel or see any differences?

If there appear to be no differences, leave the two setups (one exposed and one covered) for two more weeks, then check again.

ACID RAIN

The Earth is a huge "cup" that holds about 330 million cubic miles (1.38 billion cubic km) of water. However, 97 percent of the water is found in the Earth's salty seas and is unfit for drinking or for plants that grow in soil. Fortunately, a trillion tons of virtually salt-free rain falls on the Earth's surface every day. Four trillion gallons (16 billion tons,) of this rain fall on the United States. Rain provides the water that makes life on land possible, for water is the basic ingredient of the very flesh of which we are made. This same water evaporates from our skin and from leaves, lakes, and oceans as a vapor that enters the Earth's air only to condense and fall again as rain. The molecules of water that fall to Earth today are the same ones that fell on the backs of dinosaurs millions of years ago.

When fossil fuels burn, the impurities in these fuels combine with oxygen to form oxides of sulfur and nitrogen that pollute the air. During the 20th century, the gases released from industrial smokestacks have added increasing amounts of sulfur and nitrogen oxides to the Earth's air. These gaseous oxides combine with water vapor to form fine droplets of acid that are carried to Earth in raindrops. Such rain, called acid rain, is now common in areas over which the prevailing winds carry— for hundreds of miles—the gases released by smokestacks.

Acidity is measured in terms of pH. Pure water has a neutral pH of 7. Acidic substances, such as vinegar and lemon juice, have a pH of less than 7. Basic (or alkaline) substances, such as baking soda and household ammonia, have a pH greater than 7. You may be surprised to learn that rain normally has a pH between 5 and 6. This is because carbon dioxide in the atmosphere dissolves in the raindrops to form a weak acid. In the next three experiments you'll measure the pH of rain and see what effect it has on seeds and plants.

Experiment 14:
The pH of Rain

To find the pH of rain, let some rain fall into an open jar. Then test it by dipping a piece of pH paper (available from scientific supply houses or your school's chemistry lab) into the rainwater. Compare the color of the test paper with the color code for pH that accompanies the pH paper. What is the pH of the rain water you collected? Was the rain you collected acid rain? (A pH of less than 5.5 is considered to be acid rain.) Can you find rain that has a pH as low as that of a glass of cola?

What is the pH of vinegar? What is the pH of vinegar diluted with water (1 part vinegar to 9 parts water)? (You'll use vinegar to "water" some of the seeds and plants in Experiments 15 and 16.) What's the pH of tap water?

You may have heard that acid rain can slowly destroy statues, buildings, and gravestones made of marble or limestone. To see why, place a few marble or limestone chips in a glass. Then pour some vinegar onto the chips. What happens? What eventually happens to the solid material if you continue to add vinegar?

Experiment 15:
The Effects of Acid Rain on
the Germination of Seeds

To see the effects of acid rain on seeds, place a folded paper towel in each of three containers that can be covered. Label the containers 1, 2, and 3. On each towel place a few corn, radish, and bean seeds, as shown in Figure 10. To the seeds in container #1, add enough undiluted vinegar to make the towel moist. Moisten the towel under the second set of seeds with the diluted vinegar from Experiment 14. Use tap water to moisten the towel in container #3. (If your tap water contains chlo-

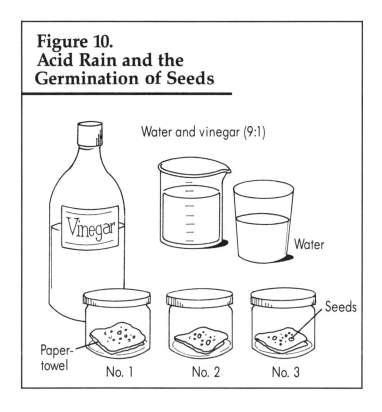

**Figure 10.
Acid Rain and the
Germination of Seeds**

Water and vinegar (9:1)

Vinegar

Water

Seeds

Paper-towel

No. 1   No. 2   No. 3

rine, let it sit in an open jar for several days so that the chlorine will escape.) The vinegar corresponds to very acidic rain. The diluted vinegar is like a less acidic rain, and the tap water is similar to normal rain.

Loosely cover each container and then check the seeds every day. The towels should be kept damp with the same liquids that were used to moisten them originally. Watch the seeds to see which ones germinate first. Are any of the seeds affected by the acid rain? How are they affected?

Experiment 16:
The Effects of Acid Rain
on Growing Plants

Plant a couple of bean or corn seeds in each of three large pots that contain potting soil. Label the pots 1, 2, and 3. Keep the soil moist with tap water until the plants have germinated and are growing well. Then begin to water pot #1 with vinegar, pot #2 with diluted vinegar (9 parts water to 1 part vinegar), and pot #3 with tap water. How do the plants compare after a week? After a month? After two months?

EARTH'S WATER

The Earth's water is polluted by chemicals that seep into groundwater or rivers. These chemicals include insecticides, oil, chemical wastes from factories, fertilizers used by farmers, leaky underground storage tanks, liquid (leachate) from landfills, and many other sources. These forms of pollution are serious problems that require sophisticated solutions. In this section we will focus on a more basic problem, the limited amount of water available to us.

You may have heard that there's a water shortage. But how can that be? The total amount of Earth's water doesn't change. Although water constantly evaporates from the oceans, lakes, forests, and grasslands, it all falls back to Earth as rain. However, as we learned in Chapter 1, the number of people who use that water continues to increase. Those same people also often waste water. In many cities, the water pipes are in such disrepair that more water is lost through leaks than is used by consumers. Feeding more people requires more water to grow more crops. It takes 15 to 20 tons of water to generate one pound (0.45 kg) of beef; 10 to 20 tons to produce one bushel (0.036 cubic m) of corn; and 120 gallons (454 L) to provide one egg.

Furthermore, rain does not follow the crowds. Those who live in lands bathed by sunlight require lots of water, but the water often has to be piped in from distant sources. In the southwestern United States, the water allocated for use from the Colorado River exceeds the volume that flows within its banks. Many parts of the United States are desperate for water. Although most doubt that it can be done, there are plans to pipe water under the ocean from Alaska to California.

WATER WASTERS

Everyone can conserve water. It's one way to help ensure that all of us have enough water for essential purposes. A home with leaky faucets, toilets, or shower heads allows thousands of gallons of water to be lost every year. This unused water simply flows to a sewer system. Experiments 17 to 22 and Projects 10 to 13 will help you to understand how water is wasted in different ways.

Experiment 17:
Checking for Leaks

To see if your home has water leaks, try this. First check to be sure that all faucets, showers, and any other water-using devices are turned off. Then, if you have a water meter, write down the meter reading on a piece of paper. Be sure that no water is used in the house for the next several hours. (This is probably easiest to do at night, when everyone is in bed.) Then read the meter again. If the meter has not changed, there are no leaks in your house. If it has changed, water is leaking somewhere in your house.

If you don't have a water meter, you probably have your own water supply. Generally, a pump is used to move the water from a well or spring to a tank in your house. Deep wells have the pump in the well. Most shallow wells have the pump in the house's basement. Check the pressure gauge on the pump or tank and watch it while someone is drawing water or while water is being used for washing clothes or dishes. You'll see the water pressure drop as water is drawn from the tank. Pumps are set to go on when the water pressure reaches a certain low level. Note the pressure at which the pump goes on. Even if it's a deep well pump, you may be able to hear it through the pipe that comes from the pump to the tank. If not, you'll know it's on when the pressure starts rising.

Now that you know the pressure at which the pump turns on, you're ready to do the experiment. When the water pressure is close to the pressure at which the pump turns on, make sure that all the faucets and other water-using devices are turned off. Wait for an hour or two and from time to time look at the pressure gauge. Does the pressure drop, causing the pump to go on? If it does, water must be leaking somewhere in your house. If it doesn't, then your house is free of any significant leaks.

Experiment 18:
Looking for Leaky Faucets

It's pretty easy to find faucets or shower heads with serious leaks. Just watch the devices for a few minutes. Do drops of water fall out? If they do, tell a parent that you know where water is being wasted in your home.

To show your parent how much water is being wasted, place a measuring cup under the faucet. Write down the time that you put the cup under the faucet or shower head. Then write down the time when the dripping water filled the measuring cup to the 1-cup (8-ounce) line. (If you use a metric cup, measure at 250 mL.) How long did it take for the water to leak from the faucet?

Liquid Volume Equivalents

English units*			metric units**
2 cups = 1 pt.		=	473 mL = 0.473 L
4 cups = 2 pt. = 1 qt.		=	946 mL = 0.946 L
16 cups = 8 pt. = 4 qt. = 1 gal.		=	3,785 mL = 3.785 L

* pt. = pint, qt. = quart, gal. = gallon   ** mL = milliliter, L = liter

Use the table to determine how much water would leak from the faucet in one day (24 hours). How much would leak in one week? In one year?

Experiment 19:
Looking for Leaky Toilets

It's not so easy to detect leaky toilets, but they're common water wasters. To see if a toilet is leaking, carefully remove the lid from the tank. Be sure to tell a parent what you plan to do. Add some food coloring to the water in the tank and stir. Wait a few minutes, and then look into the toilet bowl. If the water in the bowl is colored, then water is leaking from the tank. Your parent may be able to make a small adjustment that will stop the leak.

Experiment 20:
How Much Water Per Flush?

Modern, ultralow flush toilets use only about 1.5 gallons (6 L) per flush. But most toilets use about 6 gallons (23 L). Ask a parent if you can find out how much water the toilet or toilets in your house use per flush. To find out, all you have to do is measure how much water the tank holds. You can do that by siphoning the water into empty milk containers or several buckets. Spread some newspapers or a towel on the floor so that any water that spills will be absorbed. *Then turn off the valve in the pipe that brings water to the tank.* If you don't, water will keep pouring into the tank as you try to empty it!

To siphon the water you will need about a 4-foot (1.2-m) length of rubber or soft plastic tubing. Coil the tubing as shown in Figure 11, and hold it under the water in the tank. You'll see and hear bubbles of air coming out the upper end as the tubing becomes filled with water. When the bubbles stop, the tubing is filled with water. At that point, pinch both ends of the tubing. Have a parent, brother or sister, or friend hold one end of the tubing under the water in the tank. Keep the other end of the tubing pinched tightly shut as you bring it out of the tank and place it above the opening of a jug or bucket on the floor. The end of the tube outside the tank must be lower than the end at the bottom of the tank. When you release the end of the tubing, water will flow from the tank to the jug or bucket as shown in Figure 11. Be sure the other end of the tubing is held at the bottom of the tank. If you're collecting the water in milk jugs, quickly transfer the end of the tubing to a second jug when the first one is filled. Continue to collect water until no more flows from the tank. How many gallons or liters of water did the tank hold? How much water is used each time the toilet is flushed?

Figure 11.
Measuring Toilet Tank Capacity

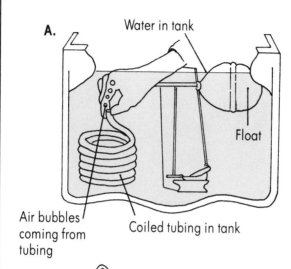

A. Water in tank

Float

Air bubbles coming from tubing

Coiled tubing in tank

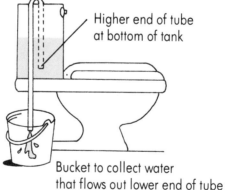

B. Higher end of tube at bottom of tank

Bucket to collect water that flows out lower end of tube

Siphon water from toilet tank to see how much water the tank holds.

Don't throw the water away. Pour it back into the tank and repeat the experiment. But this time slowly raise the end of the tube outside the tank until it is higher than the end in the tank. Why do you think the water stops flowing?

Now pour all the water back into the tank and *then* open the valve you turned off before.

Project 10:
Amount of Toilet Water
Flushed Per Day

Now that you know how much water is used each time the toilet is flushed, you can figure out how much water is used in flushing the toilet each day. You can ask each member of the family to keep track of how many times daily he or she flushes the toilet. Or you can place a notepad and pencil near the toilet. Ask everyone who uses the toilet to make a check mark on the notepad each time the toilet is flushed. How many times a day is the toilet flushed?

Multiply the number of times the toilet is flushed in one day by the number of gallons used per flush. This will give you the total amount of water used to flush the toilet in one day. For example, suppose the toilet is flushed 20 times and uses 5 gallons (19 L) with each flush. Then the water used per day is:

$$\frac{5 \text{ gal.}}{\text{flush}} \times 20 \text{ flushes} = 100 \text{ gal.}$$

How many gallons of water are used to flush this toilet each year?

Project 11:
Reducing Water Used for Toilets

You may have heard that you can conserve water by placing bricks in a toilet tank. Don't do it! The grit from the brick will cause the tank and its contents to deteriorate. What you *can* do is fill plastic quart or liter bottles with sand or pebbles. Screw on the caps and place them in the tank. Be sure that the toilet still flushes completely after the quart bottles are added. If you place two such bottles in the tank, how much less water will be needed to flush the toilet? How much water will you save in a day? In a year?

You might also buy a dam like the one in Figure 12. It's made to fit your toilet tank. It will prevent water from entering about one third of the tank, if it doesn't leak.

Experiment 21:
Bath or Shower?

Which uses more water, a bath or a shower? Most people will tell you that taking a bath uses more water. But it depends on how much time you spend in the shower.

You can easily measure the amount of water you use to take a bath. Let the water run into a bucket before you empty it into the tub. If you

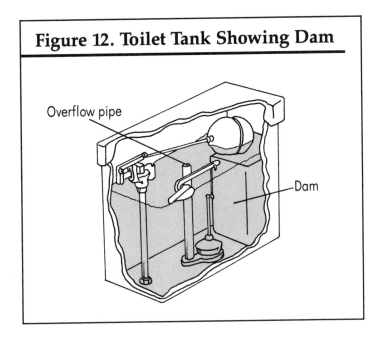

Figure 12. Toilet Tank Showing Dam

Overflow pipe

Dam

know the volume of the bucket, you can simply count how many buckets of water flowed into the tub. For example, if the bucket holds 2 gallons and you used 25 buckets in preparing your bath, then the volume of your bath water is:

$$25 \text{ buckets} \times \frac{2 \text{ gal.}}{\text{bucket}} = 50 \text{ gal.}$$

To find out how much water is used to take a shower, hold the bucket beneath the shower head while someone else measures the time it takes to fill the bucket. If it takes 30 seconds to fill a 2-gallon bucket, then 4 gallons of water come out of the shower every minute. How many gallons of water per minute come out of your shower head? How long does it take you to take a shower? How much water do you use? Do you use more water to take a bath or to take a shower? Suppose you stayed in the shower for 30 minutes: Would you use more water than you would to take a bath?

Experiment 22:
Low-Flow Shower Heads

How much water comes out of a shower head each minute? To find out, hold a pail under a shower head. Turn on the shower, and collect water for as long as it takes to nearly fill the bucket. If, for example, you collect 6 quarts in 20 seconds, you'd collect 18 quarts in a minute (60 seconds). Since there are 4 quarts in a gallon, 4.5 gallons flow from this shower head every minute. That's about normal for an ordinary shower.

Repeat the experiment with a low-flow or restricted-flow shower head. How much water per minute flows from this shower head? How does the flow of water per minute from a low-flow shower head compare with the flow from an ordinary shower head? Is it half as much? One third as much? One fourth as much? Some other fraction? How much less water do you use every minute with a low-flow shower head?

Measure the time it takes you to shower. How much water would you save if you used a low-flow shower head? How much less water would you use in a year?

In the U.S. Navy, sailors turn off the shower while they lather up to conserve fresh water, which is very precious on a ship far out at sea. How much less water would you use each year if you took Navy showers?

Project 12:
Other Water-Wasting Ways

Make an estimate of how much water is used for washing hands and faces, and for brushing teeth; for washing clothes, dishes, and cars; for watering the lawn and plants; for cooking, drinking, and making ice. Considering all the people that live in your house and all the ways water is used, about how much water is used per day in your house? If you have a water meter, you can check your estimate.

You've already seen how water can be saved by taking showers instead of baths, using low-flow showers, and reducing the water used to flush toilets. How else might you reduce water use in your home? One way would be for you to turn off the water while you brush your teeth. You could wash your hands in a basin, instead of letting the water run. You could put low-flow restrictors on your faucets.

THINK ABOUT IT. Have members of your family think about the various ways that they could reduce water use in your home. For example, how do front-loading and top-loading washers compare in terms of the water needed for their operation? Which type will help conserve water?

Project 13:
Using Rainwater

Use pails, buckets, or other containers to collect rainwater from downspouts or eaves. This water can be used in place of tap water for watering vegetable and flower gardens or houseplants.

Can you use a similar method to capture the wasted water that goes down the drain while you wait for tap water to reach a desired temperature?

THINK ABOUT IT. If you've done the experiments and projects in this chapter, you've worked hard to reduce water use in your home or school. What can you do to encourage other members of your family or your classmates to reduce the use of water? Once you succeed in getting people to reduce the volume of water they use, how can you find out how much less water is being used in your home or school?

WHAT NEXT?

In this book, we have investigated a few of the many problems that threaten the Earth. A growing population, together with a throwaway philosophy, threatens to flood the world with trash and drain away its resources and fresh water. Through the experiments and projects included here, we've found ways to combat the problems of excess solid waste. We've also investigated a number of ways to conserve water. By applying what we have learned, and by educating others, we can do our part to help save the Earth.

If you are concerned about the Earth, you will continue to investigate the many problems that face all of us who live on this planet. You will want to learn more about air and water pollution, the greenhouse effect, ozone holes in the atmosphere, energy conservation, the extinction of various plants and animals, and many other issues related to the Earth's well-being. As we've seen, Earth's problems can be solved only if people are willing to think and to change the way they live. Getting people to do either of these is a challenge. But it must happen if this fragile globe is to continue to support life in the centuries that lie ahead. We hope you'll do all you can to keep the Earth healthy.

If there is magic on this planet,
it is in water.

Loren Eiseley, "The Flow of the River"
The Immense Journey

EXPLORE THE EARTH

A Citizen's Guide to Plastics in the Ocean: More Than a Litter Problem. Washington, D.C.: Center for Marine Conservation, 1988.

Appelhoff, Mary. *Worms Eat My Garbage.* Kalamazoo, MI.: Flower Press, 1982.

Bonnet, Robert L., and Keen, G. Daniel. *Environmental Science: 49 Science Fair Projects.* Blue Ridge Summit, PA.: Tab Books, 1990.

Bramwell, Martyn. *Planet Earth.* New York: Watts, 1987.

Campbell, Stu. *Let It Rot! The Gardener's Guide to Composting.* Pownal, Vt.: Storey, 1990.

The Earth Works Group. *50 Simple Things Kids Can Do to Save the Earth.* Kansas City, MO.: Andrews and McMeel, 1990.

Gallant, Roy A. *Our Restless Earth.* New York: Watts, 1986.

Gardner, Robert. *Water: The Life Sustaining Resource.* New York: Watts, 1982.

MacEachern, Diane. *Save Our Planet: 750 Everyday Ways You Can Help Clean Up the Earth.* New York: Dell, 1990.

McLaughlin, Molly. *Earthworms, Dirt, and Rotten Leaves: An Exploration in Ecology.* New York: Macmillan, 1986.

Webster, David. *Exploring Nature Around the Year: Fall.* New York: Messner, 1989.

_____. *Exploring Nature Around the Year: Summer.* New York: Messner, 1990.

A number of valuable articles on the environment, recycling, reuse, composting, and related subjects can be found in *Garbage: The Practical Journal for the Environment.* It is published bimonthly by Old House Journal Corporation, 435 Ninth Street, Brooklyn, NY 11215. Look for it in your local library, or write for a subscription.

INDEX

Page numbers in *italics*
refer to illustrations.